Lake of Fallen Constellations

Lake of Fallen Constellations

poems

RONDA BROATCH

MoonPathPress

Copyright © 2015 Ronda Broatch

Poetry
ISBN 978-1-936657-16-2

Cover photo: "Moon and Her Lover Find the Milky Way Beneath a Skin of Water," Ronda Broatch
Author and interior photos: Ronda Broatch

Design by Tonya Namura
using Cochin

MoonPath Press is dedicated to publishing
the best poets of the U.S. Pacific Northwest

MoonPath Press
PO Box 1808
Kingston, WA 98346

MoonPathPress@yahoo.com

http://MoonPathPress.com

Acknowledgments

The author offers grateful acknowledgement to the editors of the following publications in which poems in this volume, sometimes in different form, were first published:

Adana: "After Rain"

American Poetry Journal: "Out There, the Mad Dogs Howl," "You Worry the Bear"

Atlanta Review: "How to Make Plum Dumplings"

Bellingham Review: "House of Sweet Figs," "What She Left on the Bookshelf of Another Room"

Blackbird: "Woman Goes Out into Damp December, Dish Pan in Hand"

Blood Orange Review: "Housewife Shifts Her '64 Ford Galaxie into Hyperdrive"

Blue Heron Review: "Untitled, with Valentine," "You Tell Me Happiness May Not Be Communicable"

Crab Creek Review: "Beyond the Window, Moon," "Clothespins," "The Summer I Discovered Astronomy"

Contrary: "Need Somebody to Love"

Cream City Review: "The Day I Willed His Letter to Arrive"

Diner: "How Do We Love Again This Letting Go," "There Are Things I Might Notice"

DMQ Review: "Because Even the Crows Know," "I Leave You the Cosmos," "I Want to Dissolve Into Light," "The Kitchen Witch Wanders"

Dogwood Journal: "The Other Place"

Exhibition Magazine: "Flight"

Floating Bridge Review: "The Summer I Discovered Astronomy"

Flyfish Journal: "What She Takes From the River," "Woman Dreams of Being Within"

Goldfish Press: "Words for Weather"

Ginosko: "Hand Reaching for Glass at 3 AM"

Honey Land Review: "Starting Fires Under Beds"

Hunger and Thirst Anthology: "Hunger"

The Journal: "Maybe I'm Voodoo, But I Watch," "Without Which She Isn't"

kaleidowhirl: "How Do We Love Again This Letting Go?"

Linebreak: "Anatomy of a Disaster"

Literary Salt: "Landscape with Forbidden Fruit"

Mothers and Sons Anthology: "What We Give the Skokomish"

Pacifica Literary Review: "When the Cold Names its Ghosts"

Pebble Lake Review: "I Dream a House with Many Floors"

poemeleon: "How to Make Plum Dumplings," "I Dream a House with Many Floors"

Poetry Salzburg Review: "A Bear and A Woman," "Lest a Satellite Fall to the Sea"

Pontoon: An Anthology of Washington Poets, #7: "Hunger," "What You Might Find"

Pontoon: An Anthology of Washington Poets, #9: "Housewife Shifts Her '64 Ford Galaxie into Hyperdrive," "What We Give the Skokomish"

Pontoon: An Anthology of Washington Poets, #10: "What She Takes From the River"

Quarterly West: "Sestina with Woman, with Bear"

Rattle: "Considering a Position as New Planet"

Raven Chronicles: "Grace Baking," "Instructions on Where to Find Me," "Putting the Garden to Bed"

Rougarou: "Take Bread Away From Me if You Wish"

Seattle Woman: "My Cup is a Lake of Fallen Constellations"

Segue: "Moon Shell Meditation," "Woman Emerges From Mud"

Silk Road: "Somewhere, Dog is Barking"

Smoking Poet: "All I Want is the Morning," "Postcard From the Lighthouse"

Summerset Review: "Woman Walks a Dwindling River"

Superstition Review: "In the Dark My Flashlight," "The Halo of You Was Pulled Apart"

Tiferet: "Hunger"

Valparaiso: "Reasons to Forget," "Woman Feeds on the Fragments of a Day Without Rain"

Washington Poets Anthology, 2006: "Landscape with Forbidden Fruit"

Windfall: "What She Takes From the River"

Some of these poems appeared in *Some Other Eden*, Finishing Line Press, 2005, and *Shedding Our Skins*, Finishing Line Press, 2008.

"Grace Baking" was nominated by *Raven Chronicles* for the Pushcart Prize, 2003.

"Putting the Garden to Bed" was nominated by Finishing Line Press for the Pushcart Prize, 2005.

"I Dream a House with Many Floors" was the winner of the Willamette Writers 2005 Kay Snow Poetry Award.

"What She Takes From the River" was the winner of the Washington Poets Association's William Stafford Award.

"How Do We Love Again This Letting Go" was nominated by *kaleidowhirl* for the Pushcart Prize, 2007.

"Woman Bides Her Time" was awarded Honorable Mention in the Robert Penn Warren Awards, 2007.

"I Leave You the Cosmos" was nominated by *DMQ Review* for the Pushcart Prize, 2008.

"I Want to Dissolve Into Light" (previously titled "She Wants to Dissolve Into Light" was nominated by *DMQ Review* for the Pushcart Prize, 2010.

Creation of this work was made possible in part by an Artist Trust Grants for Artist Projects (GAP) award.

Table of Contents

I.
5 Landscape with Forbidden Fruit
7 Moon Shell Meditation
8 Instructions on Where to Find Me
9 When the Cold Names Its Ghosts
10 What She Left on the Bookshelf of Another Room
11 I Want to Dissolve Into Light
13 The Summer I Discovered Astronomy
14 In the Dark My Flashlight
16 Days in Which the Sun Bled Hornets, the Earth, Wasps
19 How Do We Love Again This Letting Go?
20 Without Which She Isn't
21 I Dream a House with Many Floors
24 The Day I Willed His Letter to Arrive
26 No Ache Sweeter Than Longing

II.
29 Starting Fires Under Beds
30 Rage, the Absence of It
32 Somewhere, Dog is Barking
33 There Was a Time When Every Morning I Prayed
35 I Did Not Want to Drink the Wine or Eat the Honey
37 Anatomy of a Disaster
39 Becoming Anadromous
40 What She Takes From the River

41 Reasons for Your Forgetting
42 Clothespins
44 Maybe I'm Voodoo, But I Watch
45 The Other Place
47 Woman Walks a Dwindling River

III.

51 What You Might Find
53 Outside I Know You've Come Again
54 Hunger
55 You Worry the Bear
56 Sestina with Woman, with Bear
58 Woman Goes Out into Damp December Dish Pan in Hand
59 A Bear and A Woman
60 Because Even the Crows Know
61 This is a Language of Simple, Obvious Things
62 After Rain
64 Woman Dreams of Being Within
65 Flight
66 On the Fifth Day I Walk the North Beach

IV.

69 My Cup is a Lake of Fallen Constellations
70 Woman Feeds on the Fragments of a Day Without Rain
72 Beyond the Window, Moon
74 Considering a Position as New Planet
75 I Want to Know What Happens at the Edge of the Universe
76 Hand Reaching for Glass at 3 AM

77   What We Give the Skokomish
79   Lest a Satellite Fall to the Sea
80   Need Somebody to Love
81   Words for Weather
82   There Are Things I Might Notice
83   Out There, the Mad Dogs Howl
84   All I Want is the Morning
85   Ague
86   Grace Baking

   V.
89   The Kitchen Witch Wanders
91   How to Select an Eggplant
92   She is Peeling Apples
93   How to Make Plum Dumplings
95   Untitled, with Valentine
96   Distracted
98   Take Bread Away From Me If You Wish
100 Woman Emerges From Mud
101 House of Sweet Figs
102 The Halo of You Was Pulled Apart
103 Eve in Winter
104 Postcard From the Lighthouse
105 You Tell Me Happiness May Not
     Be Communicable
106 Housewife Shifts Her '64 Ford Galaxie into
     Hyperdrive
107 I Leave You the Cosmos
108 Putting the Garden to Bed

109 About the Author

Gratitude

Many thanks to Lana Hechtman Ayers at MoonPath Press, for her faith in my poems, her steady guidance and wisdom, and for bringing this first full collection to birth. You are amazing. Thank you to Tonya Namura for her tireless design work and editing. I'm most grateful.

Gratitude to Reverend Bill Harper, rector at Grace Episcopal Church, Bainbridge Island, who encouraged my return to poetry, and steered me in the direction of women poets, such as Mary Oliver, Lucy Shaw, and Denise Levertov; to Jim Phinney, and Bill Maxwell, those poet priests whose love of verse fanned the flame; to Ann Strickland and Susan Andersson for nurturing my work into print in those early years. And many more thank yous than I can mention here to the many talented members of Grace.

So much of this collection wouldn't have come into being without my steadfast clan of poets and friends. Special thanks to Kelli Russell Agodon, Annette Spaulding-Convy, Jenifer Browne Lawrence, Janet Knox, Natasha Kochicheril Moni, Jeannine Hall Gailey, and Holly Hughes; to Martha Silano, Anne Kundtz, and Gabriella Vogt, for their keen ideas and sharp eyes; to Ken Bennett, Susan Rich, and Rebecca Wells for their kind words; to John Willson, and to Marian McDonald, who welcomed me in to the poet fold; to my dear friend, Donna Van Renselaar, who was there when this whole poetry lark began in Nelson Bentley's beginning poetry class at the University of Washington, all those years ago. Creativity blooms wild whenever we meet.

I'm grateful to Soapstone: a Writing Retreat for Women, and to Anne Hursey, my co-resident that first snowy week of January 2004, for exchanges of stories and sketches, and shared dinners. To Centrum in Port Townsend, for more time to walk and write, in a Northwest surrounding that continues to inspire.

Heaps of thanks to my family, especially Rudy, Fiona, and Duncan, for their support and understanding of what it means to be a "poet." To my artist grandmother, Theodora, my writer grandfather, Karl, and artist father, Peter, who sparked my love of art in the first place. To my aunt, Lisbeth, for trips to plays, symphonies, museums, and other countries, and to my mother, Janet, for her belief in my work. My deepest love to you all.

And to you, dear Reader, holding this book in your hands—thank you. I hope you you find in these pages something to keep.

For Rudy, I'll always be your poet

Lake of Fallen Constellations

I

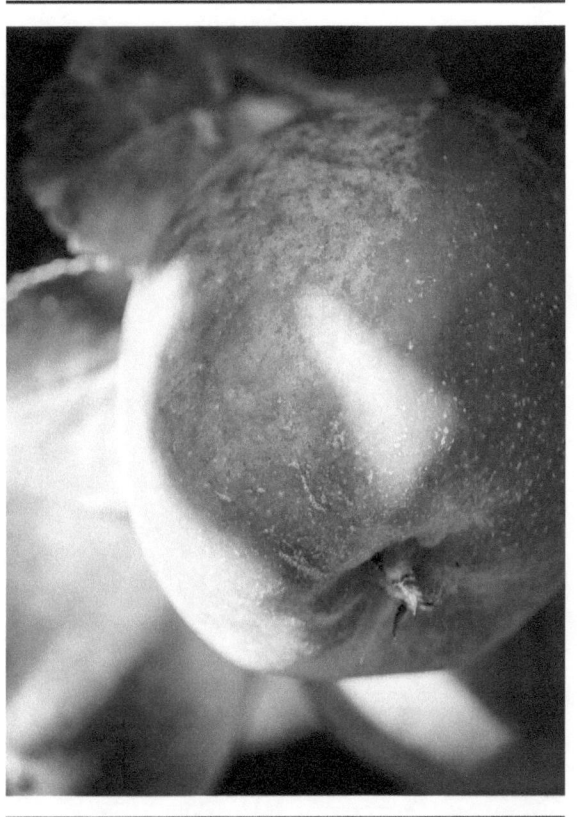

Landscape with Forbidden Fruit

    My grandmother painted naked
Adam and Eve: plans for a stained
glass window. Days when sun illuminated
    their bodies I studied

    Eve's curving apples, the curious
fruit of Adam's anatomy. My own
lean landscape green, unripe,
    unyielding of its secrets.

    Nudes I sketched in college still live
under newsprint leaves, a charcoal harvest,
abundance hidden in folios.
    And that summer in Oslo,

    when I stood transfixed
before *The Kiss*: two lovers, limbs
entangled like the leafless male and female kiwi
    vines snaking around my door:

    each entwined line etched
into copper, each body rubbed with ink,
pressed onto Fabriano cotton.
    Child of mine, what work of art

    will you steal away with,
sequestered with its sexual canvas?
Mesmerized by a rising brushstroke
    of thigh, fleshy apple breast,

    a torso's raised relief—
this is the page the book remembers,
the print hidden behind my mirror.
    You are budding

    under a meadow of skin, fresh
clay cast into slopes and valleys.
Untouched linen, tree of secrets,
    rib of new fruit—

who will draw you when you ripen?

Moon Shell Meditation

Because one in the hand looks like a breast,
its round brown nipple centered on a spiral.

Because tracing it with your fingertip
makes your heart race.

Because its long grey foot
has left it behind.

Because it reminds you of an ear —
hold it to yours.

Because even broken, your finger cannot
discover a heart,

and somewhere deep inside
it has a heart.

Because you can't see in.

Because, on the shelf, a spider
lives in it.

Because it keeps its secrets, never sleeps,
points its tiny eye to the moon.

Instructions on Where to Find Me

Today I will let my arm dangle
over an edge of the laundry basket. I'll hang
from the clothesline, my bright legs
banners for travelers and towhees.

It is arranged: my spidery hair is set
to marry the web in the garden's midst;
what wisps are left will feather
a nest of ravens. I've left

one foot in the grave
light behind the house; the other a mis-
matched sock gone beyond
where retired souls play mahjong all day.

As for my head, you'll find it
buried in a guidebook for obsolete mothers,
gardeners, and other such poets.
My organs, organized, paginated,

packaged and affixed with proper postage
await acceptance or rejection
with the exception of my heart,
which remains at home.

Have you seen my breasts?
I left them resting in the sand,
a milk-white pair of moon snail
shells caressed by the tide.

But my spirit resides in the black bear's skin,
our breath sending signals skyward.

When the Cold Names Its Ghosts

Most afternoons, I bitter tea through fields
of grief where prophets gather to feed.

The chickens have gone to roost. Soft mouthed
bears come calling. All winter

this was how I saw them. Even when floods
drowned the moon, those sibyls were out

of order, sowing wishbones along the path.
Old songs uncover thorns. Pluck these

feather-bones, pare the blood beneath my nails.
Most afternoons, I renounce everything. I am

staying forsaken, keeping a few claws in a drawer,
giving way to vagrant lovers.

What She Left on the Bookshelf of Another Room

Forget what you've left at home
for the moment. Forget the dry mouth
at night, the way waves fall
at all hours, your boots, tide-wet,

in a corner by the door. Forget the weapons
crossed on the wall of the room
in which you write, red
velvet curtains, red framed windows

across the way, the neighbor's lampshade,
red, the painting of Buddha.
In the dream is a wedding,
a young boy crying, climbing

into your lap. Open the red
heart resting on a sleeve of your sweater
by the bed. Forget Lent.
Know you're entering the sweet

Hell of chocolate and abandon by the sackful.
Document each seagull facing east
at high tide, admire beauty in the face
of the wind. Drink water from the wine

glass unrinsed, trace of the broken
Host left over, communion taken
from memory, whole yesterday, today
riddled with holes.

I Want to Dissolve Into Light

reappear
as white winter alder,
water roiling over stones. Cold,

aglow. All night I listen
as shots depart a rifle's house, ignite
a fire within the buck's breast

the river douses. The moon
a body broken, an offering
the bare floor accepts, a blessing

I circumnavigate. *Breath
cleaves from breath,
flesh from bone,*

bone from other bones. I've seen
salmon work the stones
then abandon battered

rafts of their bodies to bear,
cougar, the hungers of night.
I anchor confessions

to an antler
shed in the river's midst,
slick stones underfoot,

to grasp its ghost-white limb
with a fallen branch. Closer in,
its broken tip, a window

into marrow, I turn away.
Days I waver between flesh
and possession, weight

of blood on my hands, of bone.
Nights I lose myself
in the forgiveness of water.

The Summer I Discovered Astronomy

My neighbor is pregnant, planetary
in her red bikini. I study

the way she tends toward Mars.
Beyond her yard

in front of the brown house
I'm not allowed to enter

stands the boy who turns his eyelids
inside out for me, my heart

squirming at those shocking half moons
crimson against mahogany

skin, bare and glistening, twin
stars of his nipples quivering

as he laughs, his sister hitting him
Martín, stop it! Caught in the orbit

of his gaze, I do not walk away,
parched earth underfoot

a blazing in my belly.

In the Dark My Flashlight

makes halos, graffiti angels.
You hold fireflies in a jar,

count holes in concrete walls
like syllables to lead me on.

I navigate by fingerprint
in your wake. We discover

words, names, make sense
of hieroglyphics tattooed

in the '60s. This shirt holds sweat close
to skin; I shiver while you slice

a nectarine, take a bite, the juice of it
painting us. In the gloom,

this is just a sign, as is the motorcycle
in the parking lot beyond the lupines.

There are more forts in the woods
back of here, you tell me, grabbing

my hand. Daylight hits hard.
We squint, spines of trees grotesque

in the heat. Root and sand, mosaic
of leaves underfoot. Let's go back

to the bunkers, where it's dark,
where our phantoms live, trophies

of our recklessness. Pumice
is the only way I've found to erase

the last traces of piety
in our pockets, your hands

marble-heavy beneath my shirt.

Days in Which the Sun Bled Hornets, the Earth, Wasps

I

Here is the sting you don't remember
which you free in the shower, crimson
under nails, wings on tile.

Here is the path that winds through bramble
mist lengthening between trees, moon renewed.

II

You forget what it means
to write. Forget to write.

Forget.
Each breath

a hook for the next
breath.

III

This is the psalm,
the balm to soothe. Say it
daily, eat the wafer of relentless
Lent. What does it taste like?
Like oatmeal in the bowl
hours cold.

IV

Moored, you wish to stay
in sheets, warm, even without him
next to you. Even the blanket

stays put, your toes, warm, rags
on the floor after a week of sickness.
Ragged, like the lawn after pruning trees,

cellar of bruised apples the rats will eat.
You wish for the bear, God's hot breath
on your back, healing scars, God

a button to hold things together. God,
a pillow under knees, spine in alignment, the stars
calling you to stand out in the cold, look up.

V

In the soft partitions of sleep
you store away anxiety

parachutes packed with care. You wait
for words, wheeling

toward all you hold essential.
It's a crime to keep these alleluias

hostage in the closet.
Get married to mystery, fall

deep into honeycake, your tongue
of bees, the sweetness.

How Do We Love Again This Letting Go?

    She was a body falling
while we, with cups of tea
  and evening news, the inevitable

pull toward sateen, considered
    nothing of the possibilities
of plunging through infinity. Only

    the motion and pivot of the planets
of ourselves, our own mundane
  rotation and quaver.

We drowsed, oblivious,
    as her bright house blazed,
as with the making of a child,

    fallen godheart, offering of stars.
The moon, though wholly open,
  gave her reign to glow

for those few moments. She was
    an asteroid breaking atmosphere
at the speed of longing: headlong,

    heedless. And didn't we,
in the ether of our dreaming,
  desire to tango like that?

Without Which She Isn't

Given a choice I select
the second door. Stories of fierce

goodness rouse me. Some nights
I remember flight, immaculate

atmosphere, deciduous dreams.
Mornings arrive early,

torn and wrought with pins.
Right-handed I am drawn

left. There are times I'd climb
back into the Big Hand, remain

until the storm abates. Tomorrow
I am intensely happy. Today

I drag the sorrow bag.
Cats, attracted to my letters,

lie. *Mailbox* is another name
for hope. Without it

I am lost for words. Always
I tend toward water.

I Dream a House with Many Floors,

    more stories than my own
to explore, with a view
        above the holly tree,

    the yew.
Nights, as a child
        I flew through the living room

    and kitchen, mostly,
hair brushing ceiling.
        Often I'd soar

    out of the window, skim
rooftops, tops of firs
        and the apple wood,

    in search
of heavenly elevation.
        A midnight height

    to house
chambers like the hidden
        room behind the wardrobe,

    pale light breathing green
through a simple window
        obscured by trees.

    There,
in the treasured gloom:
        A babble of books

    in a foreign tongue.
Woolen coats in repose,
        sheathed in sheets and moth dust.

    Velvet smoothed with use,
hats lined with tattered
        thoughts trail their plumage

    to the floor.
A finch's discarded wing,
        a single black shoe.

    Discovered, they loosed
my longing for flight,
        for landings spanning

    beyond what I knew,
a God I could grasp,
        a face to hang in my attic.

    This is the updraft of words
heard before birth in the palm
        of a broad hand,

    where I sat
listening to my life.
        This is

    the place in-between,
aerie beneath the ether,
        where I can almost reach

    the apple
at the topmost limb
        before it slips—

The Day I Willed His Letter to Arrive

I reached inside
the green box   knuckles scraping
asbestos siding & felt the surge

of my influence
like a new baby
like a decoder ring   secret

password I inherited from my
mother who heard the single
ghostly note over & over

from the toy piano
high on the closet shelf   mom
in the bathtub   no one

else in the house
the same house where I watched
Saturday Night Live & the Chihuahua

that stood between the living
room & my bedroom
stood there &   *shit*

it wouldn't go away   scratching its ear
with one crazy hind leg   only I
didn't have a Chihuahua

or any dog & what about the time
my girlfriend & I said
the same word   same time

& the radio in my '65 Plymouth
Belvedere played   first time in fifteen years
but only for half a day & the day

I considered earthquakes while driving
to church on Ash Wednesday
how later the phone rang

while people sang & there was
nobody on the line   or maybe
it was God & a minute later

with the singing going on   the floor
trembled & everyone
hauled for the exits & I

wished I could slip this
gift   this heavy necklace
over my head   no

pocket it & use it again & again
like some magician   but oh
there are nights

I play movies in my head
see my children my husband my life
in ways I…

I close my eyes
& tell God   *no*
like this

No Ache Sweeter Than Longing

Did I mention I went out, put on the rough garden
shoes I've had since our youngest was small. Still
they hold my feet like faithful dogs with soft

mouths. The pond appeared within the winter
meadow, and a pair of Canada geese argued
kar - uunk, *kar - uunk*, twisting molten glass

black necks. Because I came to see them they rose
from the pond's burning surface, the vees of
their bodies drawing toward Puget Sound.

How the aging light loves their wingtips. I say to you,
the waves strayed farther from the cliffs this evening
so the rocks could breathe. As she fell toward water

the sun bled. Moon opened her blue robe halfway.
It was the eagle who watched it all unfold.
From him no secrets are hid.

As I came to stand beneath
him, high on a madrona bough,
he lifted into the sun.

II

Starting Fires Under Beds

Here is where the charcoal
nudes you sketched lie
abed with etchings on sheets

of Rives, where the neighbor boy
tried to light a fire-
cracker in the only wait-until-dark

he could find. Photos you took
of yourself, naked, in boxes
smolder. You stare

in the bathroom mirror, notice
the Rubenesqueness
of your waist, thank

the light switch. At night
you throw off blankets and layers
(another kind of conflagration)

and your husband moves
closer, attracted
like a moth. It's not light

you emit, but he knows
heat, having ignited
his own years ago.

Rage, the Absence of It

It wants to be the thumbprint
on the bride's forehead.
It wants to be the horn-gored matador.
Drained, it has no words.

Like red, you hold it on your tongue.
Because that's what remains when the tone sounds.
Because, without the matador, the bride
becomes the river she washes in.
Because it's been nearly a year.

Everything you lost.
The red fabric worn by each marked bride.
Jupiter's Great Red Spot.
Everything you didn't know you lost.
Red.   Like when you close your eyes.   Like that.

A circle.   Thirst.
(Before that.)
Thorn of Christ.
The dream of camel and bristlecone pine.
The bride's gored heart.

A new crater forms.
Someone puts on boots.
Someone plants beet seeds and tomatoes.
The lily and the rose change skins.
The dark side spreads its bitter lake, turns red.

Inside the shoes forgotten outside each door.
Inside the chocolates and the oranges and the coal.

Along the red edges of loss.
In a dusty corner of the pool table covered in felt.
The darkness beneath the bride's tiny feet.

Somewhere, Dog is Barking

                       He's the one
gone mean, keen for a jaw
snap, taste of flesh on the back
of his tongue. Sometimes God
gets bored, needs some
action, a little bone-bite-satisfaction

between his teeth.
                       Rosalie keeps
a metal stick for times like these,
deals the wind a whack or two, asks
may we walk together, as if I might
protect her. Let's change the picture,
reverse the order: Dog to God.

What happens next?
                       Rosalie trots,
her hair a cirrus wisp against blue.
Ours is son-talk, angles of carpentry
and death camps, how a family fled
to America, how a sister escaped
to Arizona, her bones too cold up here.

We cross the bridge.
                       Rosalie beats
a tattoo on rocks with her rod
while new-strung words like prayer
beads roll, rough on my tongue.
Beneath our feet Soapstone Creek
feeds ravenous Nehalem's North Fork

                     and we never once
meet Dog.

There Was a Time When Every Morning I Prayed

to denim sky and Steller's jays piercing

the birdbath's frozen glass.
O please let there be –

Time was when I could awaken
within the apricot

some brightness no pit would diminish.
When I might step from bed

to bedlam and not buckle beneath.
Some things fray beyond need for thread,

where we ribbon together twig and herb,
place bones in the breadbox. Once I found

the vertebra of a deer, empty body
of bourbon beckoning spider and ant.

Yearning for adverbs, I discard them
when simple is sought.

I repeat and repeat the way my horse
returns to stable day after day,

each day more quickly home.
Now the apricot tree's in bloom, now

the plum. Next thing we're buckling
children into car seats, placing marigolds

over eyes of the withered
stepping from bedlam to bed.

What if I could breathe into my palm,
let the seeds float otherwhere?

What if we were weightless, thin
as smoke? The Steller's jay points its beak

threads woodsmoke and winter.
I gravy the soup, add peas last of all

to keep them bright. Chickadees are first
to arrive, last to leave, little wings

and adverbs. Flitter, flitter, flitter.
There is no glass

no bourbon left. I wish to float
while children yet strain at their bonds,

while the bickering continues like song
behind the seat. This life

has its wings and repeats, apricots, bourbon
and woodsmoke. Just once let me be

the round eye of the marigold
dead center.

I Did Not Want to Drink the Wine or Eat the Honey

I have eaten my honeycomb and my honey; I have drunk my wine and my milk. Eat, O friends, and drink; drink your fill, O lovers.
—Song of Solomon, 5:1

Splinter is another name for distraction between us
when the woodstove's gone cold.
We wait a year to feed the baby

honey, a few more to give her wine,
deem the green paint too green, that vines
might be stenciled against it, but in the dim

everything disappears. Mornings it seems
my to-dos congregate like lemmings
and all I've collected falls.

We build a shrine of newspapers,
to the gods of the cross-
word, to a life of brevity,

to *How red should this wall be* when we finally break
its façade. Absolutely naught
would have been better than to sink into sheet-

rock, spill over cliff, listen to laugh
of the swineherd. In this year of dying I slack
into bathrobe, tomorrow, fingerprints

on glass. I rub hard each day
to remove the day, look to the hillside
where are buried the torsos of trees,

dead of past fires. After the body
steeped in balsamic and finest virgin,
this water is the best I've tasted,

having given up so much of its blood
for honey.

Anatomy of a Disaster

Call yourself crazy, but these swallows in the eaves speak
of arriving, of settling in like flames.
                    It is midnight when you flee

with your daughter into the garden, blessing
a nursing bra, holey pair of panties. How you stare,
    amazed
  as people grow from the ground, shimmering

in tuxedos to praise the raging body
of your home, gaping
  windows keeping nothing sacred. Morning you return,

                              home a post-
holocaust sanctuary, plastic curtain grafted to the altar
of your vanity. You see in the sodden marriage

of your photos a glue no prying will undo: wife to
    husband,
the mouth of your child an O against the ear of a relative
  whose name escapes you. All next year

you dream of flight, of burning and birth,
a looseness. You sleep longer,
    wandering

                    among the ashes where you haunt
the ghosts of your belongings: knitting needle stuck
to the baby's doll, hearts of sweaters eaten by mice.

You admire charred trees their audacity
to reach beyond earth, think of planting beans,
    of attaining heaven
  by climbing. You pine for simpler things,

whole days outside. Blood, as a method
of expression, not a map of your years. In the soil,
   eyes burning, you find another shard

of glass — pollen, or the low morning sun —
you've no time to question, what with these seeds
   to tamp down, one more year rushing by

        like a house on fire.

Becoming Anadromous

Who needs fire? We are two kinds of water, you in aqua
marine tuxedo, and I in a freshwater dress,
skimming floor once more before they pull the plug,

send us swirling down dawn, trail of oil rainbowing
beneath your bike. I'll learn to lean into you,
how to ride out an earthquake

in your bed, the scent of melons sending us sleepwise.
    Seismic
is what we call ourselves, tsunamis, cliff jumpers missing
for weeks. It's no surprise we've become shoeless, naked

with all that walking, all this steam. Vapor is vapor,
but the language of lines raked in earth speaks
of Yellow Finns and beets, of fence lines, foundations:

all things rooted. Give me your feet. I'll fill a bowl with
river, with dirt, my thumbs divining your Achilles heel.
If the tide charts are true

we'll find a way to come together, when the land bridge
returns, once every never. I'll fill five canvases
with Atlantic and Cutthroat, you'll write your field guide

to bladder wrack and kelp. Contrary
to popular belief, we're connected, Chinook living on
in the sea for years before returning.

What She Takes From the River

I fry onions, add asparagus, a few
green tips mingling with a touch of pink
from last night's dinner. Chinook

spawn downstream, a female and two males—
the same three this past week.
Because this is new to me I retreat

to the river daily, watch the males muscling,
sinewy, sinuous, next moment
motionless, aligned with the current.

The female fans a redd. Tentative
I shift, watch her drift, dart back
to nose in under a branch

above the antler I discovered
yesterday, when we spooked each other,
my dark form looming predatory,

her body arrowing over black rock
into deeper water. Now exposed,
I fish for the horn with a twig,

claim it for my own until broken tips
and blood-tinged grooves
come into view. Shimmy it upright,

let it rest. Come night I awaken,
the moon a new-cut onion,
open and raw.

Reasons for Your Forgetting

Sometimes you remember your anniversary
a week later, marvel at how you've moved on.
It is the year of rabbits and deer, of coyotes

encroaching. The house different now, its downstairs
kitchen, living room where the cars were parked.
You've left the bedroom where it was, bed

facing east instead of west, yet there've been no more
flames. You think you've fulfilled some rite of passage,
entered the right password enabling you to stay

these seventeen years beyond burning.
    Raspberries greening,
apples trees in tentative blossom. This is the moment
of deep-seeded hunger, week of planting

carrots, beans and beets, a keenness you know
you'll cure if the sun persists, if the soil gives
a little more. Digging, you examine shattered

windows, bits of charcoal, whole trunks
charred, feeding the earth. You weren't the first
to burst into blaze, won't be the last.

Clothespins

I found some clothespins today,
in the short and brownish grass,
fallen from lines after last week's snow.

During the cold months they appear
around the house, little wooden hints
under the spinning wheel,

in old yogurt cups, one pin in each,
along with a Lego or two,
and some plastic beads.

I discovered God the same way,
behind the house in bright April
laundry flying on the lines.

I began thinking about spring,
about hanging out the clothes —
I get so distracted now

the honey-moon is over. No more sleep-
less midnights catching up on Holy Spirit.
No piercing illuminations

while driving the kids to school.
Life is leaking back to normal;
fingers drum on the table once again,

reminding me that my pile of laundry
grows without concern for my spiritual life,
there are dishes to be scrubbed,

my daughter's report, due tomorrow.
Bulbs desiring soil sprout
in paper bags beside the door.

Time to hang my life on the line
to air. Shake out the grievances and stale worries.
Freshen the soul with compassion,

some last-minute forgivenesses, and
I was just thinking…
Now would be a good time to get the Alleluias out.

Maybe I'm Voodoo, But I Watch

pots to prove them wrong, copper & stained
La Paella, skin-chipped *Le Creuset*.
Know, given heat given time,
the watched pot will.
                         I note

the resurrection between flat line
and roiling, the point at which
skin blisters, steamed or broiled, the hand
wrapped around a fry pan's handle
                fresh from the oven,

the way ice water shocks
further cooking. I prick myself
with blackberry thorns, get to the heart
of the patch, to the juice & pulp of the matter,
                        still lucid after cracking

egg into bowl, top of my head
under cupboard door. But more than that
I'm a doll, soft with pins,
meridian model looking to needle
              my chi, back to its canvas, chanting

> *A stick in the heel to hobble your wandering,*
> *one in the ear to cobble your thoughts,*
> *one to pierce the map of the heart*
> *to show me*
> *where you last fell in.*

The Other Place

You visit while walking,
    or taking tea, or reading
        and it is autumn.
Sun sips crimson from the liquid
    amber tree and you

        are standing at the edge
    of a meadow steeped
in a flaxen light. You might like
        to step in, your heart,
    fledgling bird, quickening to fly

to that yellow house
    on the hill — but always
        she appears before you,
weaving in the blue
    shade you've become

        accustomed to.
    What toll to pay to gain safe passage?
An unsung ballad, a blackbird coat,
        pockets laden
    with riddles and bones.

In the pale morning, a raven swallows
    voices of the dead.
        When the wind is thin you hear her
croaking instructions
    as if death was just

       another skin.
    Something slithers
away in translation.
       Something slips
into focus: leaves

quivering at the fringe,
    the body you gave to the river,
        shoes on the bank, waiting.
The book turns its own pages.
    The empty cup.

       And what of this sudden chill,
    these feathers clutched to your breast?
You remember your breath.
       You find it painful
    not to sing.

Woman Walks a Dwindling River

these limbs knocking windows
   this wind

this parched mouth
   this drought

rain tied back in grey drapes
   one nudge

and the whole jerry rigged mast
   will collapse

this flood   these saturated shoes
   puncture wound

induced by walking   the ruined foot   this
   journey inter-

rupted to patch holes   this broken boat
   these weeds

fish weaving in   the quiet mud
   this sucking

slow exhale   this pull toward
   sleep   this

nightshift   this turning

III

What You Might Find

On the pretense of retrieving
              something forgotten,
   you find yourself

      standing by the bird feeder.
      A disturbance of leaves,
sudden shake of shrubs
      draws you away from your task.

      You're certain it's him,

can almost see his curved form
     disappear through the elderberry brush.
     You want him to stop,

      rise on hind legs
      as he scents your presence,
   hear the sharp intake and exhale
           of his breath.

You go to the edge,
    separate the dry bones of foliage,
       desire blooming in your breast.

      And he is here,
ambling forward, as if time was
     long as his winter shadow.

      Slowly he turns, addresses you, fully
god-tall, blinding bright.
    Shielding your eyes against him,
       against his advancing truth,
     shaking as he drapes you in his great heat —

Then nothing.

No weight,
        no breath but the wind.

You feel your nakedness for the first time,
    tremble alone under thrush song,
            alive
                in your skin of bear.

Outside I Know You've Come Again

Whole seasons   I divide
from you

reside   in this bodi-
less silence

while homeless
you roam

clatter your hoary bones
You say

you wish to mend me
stitch

the distance between us
steal

my skin   while I sleep
In this lean

time   no feeding
from garden fruit

So give me light
on the half   moon

while winter drips
into spring

a hint   of green tips —

nothing yet into which
we may sink our teeth

Hunger

In the middle night
I forage for food to steal
the edge of sleep.

                              Moon is an eggshell
                      above migrating cloud, a glow
             by which the banished bear roves.

Chickens have turned to stone
dogs are mad with barking.
I wait on the other side of glass

                                  dry bread in hand
                                water to sustain me.
                              Sometimes the bear

is God moving
in and through my life.
Ravenous he breaks me

                                open like fruit,
                        consumes me wholly.
            I climb through the night window

his name burning my throat
like wine, hunger
connecting us

                                  wind searching
                              for something it has
                                not yet touched.

You Worry the Bear

a dog drawn to its meat
missing the imagined
more than reason's frost-

heaved rock on which you stumble.
Stubbed, you wake by degrees
wait again for sleep. Beneath,

the earth reeks and you
dream of spring, overturned
rock, a trap grown thickly

over. A stick to take you
through, a sign
to divine what lies

breathing, barely. Hibernation
is an ether dreamed of, an assumption
of fat and pelt. You sleep under

loam and the weight of days
living off the flesh
of what was.

Sestina with Woman, with Bear

Returning home, late, the moon
caught in alders like a blessing
someone dropped in haste to appear
in the right place, right time, the woman
lingers in the garden, tips of peas rising
above the soil. Times like these she bears

a hunger slowly waking. Somewhere, a bear
has woken, too. Guided by the moon,
she nuzzles her cub before rising
to quell its appetite. A blessing
these trees, this safe haven. The woman,
her want a gulf widening, appeals

to the darkness, to a god who appears
never when she needs. The bear
will ravage the compost the woman
buried beneath cedar trees, the half moon
an idea between clouds. She blesses
the soft earth, loam compliant to the rise

and fall of a pickaxe. A small pain rises
to the surface today, an ache appearing
in cycles. In this church of dirt, blessings
come disguised as craving and the bear
roves unseen through underbrush. Mooning,
her cub lags behind. Nothing the woman

completes seems done, her man
returning in two days. She rises
early, looks up *Wolf Moon, Hunger Moon,*

Moon of the Long Night. He appears
in dreams with the face of a bear,
coated in clay, his blessed

boots tramping the mat. The sun bleeds
into day and heavy with seed the woman
prays to her never-god, a barren
plea. Beyond the garden, over rise,
the bear looks on, Sated, he disappears.
Planter's Moon, Awakening Moon, Moon

of the Long Wait. Moored, she is blessed
by such appearances. In dreams the woman
rises in the night and feeds the bear.

Woman Goes Out into Damp December Dish Pan in Hand

offers water to the slumbering
    blackberry vines. Slaps the pan,
        imagines the bear,

come round two mornings before,
    wrought iron pole of the bird house bowed
        nearly double. She conjures

the great black shape,
    belly full of suet, chickadee
        feeder broken at his feet, perches

neatly removed, plastic tube pierced
    by the tooth of his hunger. She's seen
        where he hunkers, straw of dying

grass flattened in the woods
    behind her home, nocturnal swath
        carved wide with his wanderings.

She wants to catch him at his tricks,
    wonders if she were to yield
        her last basket of apples—

mealy, sweet—if giving brings more
    than a bearish appetite.
        In this slim, growing bleak

and dusky hour, she greets
    a moon swelling with secrets, a body
        pressing on through darkness.

A Bear and A Woman

There has always been a bear, a woman,
each navigating by her own
set of stars, a common moon. The woman

lies in bed while her children roam
from room to room to kitchen.
The bear sends her cubs

to the compost heap, then
watching them gorge, approaches,
cuffs them away. Days, the woman

waits at wood's edge, claw of moon
in the maple. Her unknowingness traps her.
The bear sees her,

moves on.

Because Even the Crows Know

You shut the book,
wait for the voices to die.

There is only space,
crows filling it, the wind

blowing dust from the maple's many hands.
Dry August. In the grass

you espy something shiny.
But the sun keeps walking

and it seems you were wrong.
Because the shade plays

tricks on the afternoon light
you are not convinced.

The crows know,
and they've stopped talking.

This is a Language of Simple, Obvious Things

—after a line by Anna Moschovakis

how the wife cuts asparagus into lengths
the steamer will accept, how the husband
clears the table of bills, expired

subscriptions the wife collects. She pulls
potatoes out of the oven, broils
her knuckles—just briefly—

while the husband draws knives, forks,
from their slotted beds, plunks them
on the scrubbed pine where books of poetry, odes

to joy and mammography
reminders rest in a neat stack at its head.
The wife carves the roast, drops a slice

onto a blue platter with orange
carrots the husband awakes from someplace
just beneath reach of the sun.

After Rain

On days like this you sink into muck
thick as paint, mesh sneakers filling, socks
scrunched down around toes. Under rocks

you find the idea of a chameleon,
but never the real thing. You wish
to live in a world where asphalt

is an afterthought, where balloons swim
overhead, but don't frighten the horses, huff
of air and volume rising. You have no use for

the bathrobe hanging on the door, put on
what you wore before your shower. It's been years
since you've spun, your wheels gathering dust

in the bedroom, your wheels spinning
when you most need sleep. And isn't that
what everyone says, falling into spring,

watching winter slip away under-
appreciated. Green fingers on the clematis,
a smudge on every window, you want what burns

in the oven, the smell of pecan or almonds,
voice of Sekou Sundiata an island
amidst a hectic afternoon. You ask

the seaplane that circled above, and plummeted
just yards above your car, to replay its stunt,
wake you up, want the pilot's

eye on you. In frescos of cedar bark you see
criticisms, misplaced seed of your creativity.
Is goodbye the last line, or is there another

sound to string you along? Rain abated,
this cloudy mouth of sky holds no traffic. Loam
beneath your feet a sponge, you are suspended. Close

your eyes, imagine inhaling up and over the crest
of your being. Wish to be water, to be well,
clear enough to see inside.

Woman Dreams of Being Within

I am the fish
in the bear's mouth

silver wriggling rainbow

my broken body a sacred house
for his blameless tongue

There is beauty in the draping curve of death

He will follow the driven river
and I inside him will break apart

swim into arteries   muscles   organs   pores
whole in this new ocean

Flight

The
    early
       morning
          was a nameless
             bird scattering feathers
                across the icy mirror of the bay
                    and a bit of pigment seeped away from
                    each vane staining the water
                purple crimson amber grey
           in her reckless haste to paint
        the sky and I wonder—
what will be left of her
when she finally
    finds
     the
      w
      e
      s
      t
      ?

On the Fifth Day I Walk the North Beach

An eagle settles in the madrona
between the moon and me,
while sun bleeds over the Olympics.
I have just seen the meaty wing of a seagull.

I imagine rolling over sand.
It's almost dusk, and the coyotes
have eaten the moon's darker face.

Show me again the Big Dipper
has everything to do with earth's
great thirst. I am burying
my transgressions.

Understand the eagle has a lesson in solitude.
Understand sunset has enslaved lovers.
Understand the seagull's wing once drew the stars
into being.

IV

My Cup is a Lake of Fallen Constellations

You say *I will be with you always*
but this silence is a dry mouth,
an ear that bends to imagining
the wind has gone.

Possibility walks away with strangers,
opening windows, closing them.
Retreats unseen to the ocean,
leaves no boat to sail,

drips through my thinning fingers.
You tell me it is bread on my tongue,
your body melting in mine, red wine
I drown in. Your words

like water under my feet.
Say there are more stars
in the well tonight. Pour
a galaxy into my hand,

number each luminous body
burning my palm, give it a name.
I'll stand on the shore, thirsty,
waiting for wind to rise.

Woman Feeds on the Fragments
of a Day Without Rain

When the nuthatch lights
   in limbs of the fig,
      I fill

clam shells with water
   to slake its thirst,
      watch it sip

from drops on leaves
   meant to bless the young
      tree, hoping

it will hold
   its small figs forming.
      I see them

ripening, know the fleshy
   redness of uterine fruit.
      Pregnant

evening deepens, nuthatch
   sleeps, moon swells
      in a cirrus sea.

Coyote roams her road, raccoon
   follows her hunger,
      chickens and cats

shed their lives
    to feed the ravenous
        rotation that lures them,

    tides they cannot survive
        without.

Beyond the Window, Moon

is a white eye nearly open.
Behind the black-
berry jungle, frog song cracks
like knuckles, and owl forgets
the names of everyone she ever knew.

Bear noses the worm bin
for moldy bread and eggs shells,
as raccoons scale the chicken house,
peeling sheets of roofing
away like skin.

Coyote lines her belly
with hides of banished cats.
Another hound
tied to the clothesline
unites its choking coda to the chorus.

I might leap from this window,
join the beasts of night, imagine
myself already rising from the bed,
my sleek furred body
quivering on the ledge,

electric with possibility—
but in you slip,
soundless through the room,
shut the window with a slide—
and we are within, alone

in the lamplight,
the discarded skins
of our clothing on the floor,
huff of our animal breath enough
to hush the maddening din.

Considering a Position as New Planet

                I envy them
           their silent lines
            suggestive trajectories —
      such an elegant
      loneliness there
     in the heavenly murk.
    Who could help
   but answer the appeal
  let go a toe-
 hold and rise
through atmosphere
out to where
ascension becomes
 suspension and revolution.
What would happen
  once fuel runs low —
    Would we wither, shivering
      past banished Pluto
        or just go on skipping
          in perfect ellipses
            until we find ourselves
              melting, a tender bread
                on the sun's tongue?

I Want to Know What Happens at the Edge of the Universe

that dark mouth holding us all
in its teeth. Let me see

what the neighbor does within the walls
of his little grey house, the one

by four crucifix nailed to the T-
one eleven siding, upside

down on Easter. The body
(baggy jeans and sweatshirt, a balloon

stuffed hood) flew the coop
last night. When she heard her son

was dealing meth, his mother served
eviction on a clipboard,

two officers on the side. And I
want to know if he's ever looked at the moon

much less the stars. And whether he too
has tilted

his head back to catch
just   one

brilliant
body.

Hand Reaching for Glass at 3AM

The child clamors for drink,
cracks the vessel of sleep.

> The rain wants in,
> while the window, indifferent,

knows no thirst.
A shell, upturned, cups

> ocean to its ear. Empty
> it speaks of rejection.

One face of glass beads sweat,
the other denies water's existence.

> The tongue speaks for the parched body.
> (Breath cleaves to breath.)

The hand divines water in darkness,
opens dreams.

> Sleep rubs against itself
> and anxiety is born.

How sleep cleaves to sleep,
then peels away.

> Mother and child,
> skin of bark. These too,

(if woven tightly)
> hold water.

What We Give the Skokomish

Red sandstone heaved
   from beneath earth diverts

the river's flow, carries my son's boat

   past his grip.
      He retreats between fir trees

to camp, to search

   for feather-light wood, twigs
      for rigging, maple leaf sails.

I remain here, the warm rock,

   my own stone pump
      bumping and tumbling within its confines

to rapid music, an aberrant

   current I can't seem to master.
      You have premature atrial contractions.

Palpitations. *Could be hormones,*

   medication, anxiety, stress. My heart
      is a vessel swelling with terms —

so many names, so many words.

   My son returns, a new raft in hand,
      crafted from cedar and fir —

he sets it adrift. Eyes closed

    I absorb the river's sucking rush,
        one artery pulsing seaward.

Lest a Satellite Fall to the Sea

you bring teasels indoors, a lilt
in your step, slate tiles and sleet
underfoot. I'm squeamish, face East

mornings for a better perspective. Elate the easel
relate tales that steal the senses as I taste
salt in the tea you make. Latte

is another word for awake, is another way to tease
I love you, but from a distance. We'd never attest
to Seattle, and I don't want to sail

there with you. The sea fills these halls, but at least
we'll settle our estate, Sat. at the very latest,
before the eels seal our view. You list

titles on my bookshelf the way I quote Tesla. Stale
conversation, tales of ale and onions. A tattle
of lies we keep beneath the seat.

Need Somebody to Love

I've picked each fruit under prickly dark leaves,
planted my Queen of the Night,

and now this sliver of bark won't budge
for love, money, nor squeeze

of tweezers, like the stinger that lingers
after the death of a bee. The Chablis's

gone to my head, Mercury
dead these nineteen years. I was

so sorry to see him leave. Tomorrow
it may rain. Some things arrive

on faith. Its black cap
aflame, the tulip carries its secret

sex in its mouth. Many times
I've visited this arena, have sat

at the right hand side. Tonight
I need somebody to raise

Freddie from his grave, give him back
his microphone, his white skin-tight

body suit, his love. These berries
in my bowl are cold, hold their juice

only so long. Oh thorn in my flesh, pollen
on the stamens, my wine-heavy mind.

Words for Weather

They say heat rises so we climb
to an upstairs room,
two windows watching river.
They say *serein* is French

for rain and I believe in
the speech of water as it falls,
flows and circles back to itself.
Give me something

hot and I will temper it
with *heimal, brumal, algid, keen* —
standing in the stream at February's birth.
Colder than blixens, you might say,

and I can see my naked feet, skin grey,
two sockeye eddied at the base
of the cascade. *Gully washer,
fence lifter, root searcher, deluge* —

these point the way
to *bedroom, blanket, rain-on-the-roof* —
the language of blood returning heat,
breath heavy with what we've left unsaid.

There Are Things I Might Notice

if you didn't abandon me here,
holding the stone of my imagination
like some dead weight in my pack.

If it wasn't my burden to picture
you slipping from that log that juts
twelve feet above riverbank, I might feel

July's heat on my back,
take in the arc of a perfect cast,
masts of dry grass resisting wind,

so many plants whose names
I'll later find in a field guide.
Take careful note

how along the cliff edge
fir and madrona appear like women
lined up, waiting to die,

their sisters bridging river.
How green and frigid the water,
and all these boulders.

Beneath them, fine pebbles and sand,
shoots breaking through.
And now you,

down here with me,
you, counting each stone
with the open curve of your foot.

Out There, the Mad Dogs Howl

Outside, my darling,
    the wild things prowl.
The owl rises with the wrecked mouse
   and dry grass rattles winter
      from its bones.

Out there, little thing,
    the coyotes sing
the ballad of the wandering cat,
   and the shrews you slew
      will remember you,

as beasts unseen move
     mute between quaking trees.
Tattered clouds shroud
  a moon unmade, and mad
     dogs wail.

Inside, you are
    oil slick black, slipping
seal-like on Hudson's Bay spread,
   pure pleasure of being
      allowed in my bed.

All I Want is the Morning

paper with its crossword
puzzles and funnies,
the tea in my cup
warm. All I want is sun
enough to dry the lawn,

the mower, asleep
these winter months, full
of fuel, an untamed
pasture before me, a solid
place on this hard earth.

All I want is another planet
besides this one, to know
there is life in a place
I don't know, an ocean
deeper than this, or perhaps

just a lake
surrounded by trees, grass
waving in a breeze much like
here, a girl dipping
her toes beneath the surface

for the first time
on a spring day
after reading
her first love
poem.

Ague

You say you'll mend
the kitchen sink tomorrow, stop

the drips that wake us.
I say your holey pockets will self

heal by the time you return.
The car coughs, threatens

to expire, and I can't seem to rejoin
the twin to this orphaned

alpaca sock. The hole worsens
in the stairwell wall, the tool

shed has shingles and a rash
contracted from so many Pileated

pecks. The honey's got hives
even the bear can't scratch.

I wake each morning to growls
the refrigerator makes

deep in its bowels, bone
china rattling above, ice

coating the Butterleaf,
the bread.

Grace Baking

                                      Yesterday
Jesus was a woman,
    her disheveled hair falling
from a hairnet onto square shoulders.
She bagged loaves in pairs:
        potato rosemary, pugliese, garlic — soft
whole cloves imbedded in a porous
        body of wheat.
Near the fish counter and crates of wine

we spoke of children, of school starting.
    God'll bless you, she said,
wiping floured hands on a floral apron,
    and I agreed *Amen*.
We sampled bread, skin still crackling,
warm, as she pressed bags of fresh-

baked rolls against her breasts.
    *It's the music that gets
    the menfolk to church*, she stated,
not missing a beat, slipping baguettes
into sacks marked Grace Baking on the outside.
    Grace is the name of our church,
I pointed out, and she smiled at me.

    Have some more bread, she said.

Amen.

V

The Kitchen Witch Wanders

—with a line by Rumi

sops up blood
from the counter, shoves

    cumin-smeared thighs
into the maw

of the oven
Can't get Barks reeling Rumi out
        of her mind—

    let what we love
    be what we do

Leftover noodles plump
        in copper pot
    flame on high

      let what we
love be what we do

    Drawn & quartered
Delicata forgotten

      lest we love
  what do we be

yesterday's gravy
bubbling, clotting
        dropped

into fat & stock
      a fresh roux —

      O what do we do?
We love
    we let be

How to Select an Eggplant

He's thinking torso *Rubenesque*
She suggests breaded medallions
parmigiano-reggiano

marinara so blood red, so night-
shade on the tongue
it makes her blush. *Aubergine*

he breathes, and says it again.
Crostini Chianti Balsamic
Rub a little extra virgin

Olio Verde into flesh,
make it hiss. *This one is a breast*
he says, perfect

cupped in his palm. *Better grab two*
she muses — *the moon
    is round tonight.*

She is Peeling Apples

        her large lap spread
            with a flowered
                cloth to cradle
                      apples she is paring
                        into a well-worn pot
            in the house
        apples stewing
    on the stove
apples waiting
on the porch
    in cloth bags
        apples under trees
            scattered by bears
                robin carved and circled
              by snakes, lifted
            by raccoons. She
        is seeding Spartans
    cutting Gravensteins
feeding Liberties
to her heedless children
    Summer Reds
        to her man coming
            weary through the door
                after work
                his aching rib
            mended by
        the sight of her
    and her fruits
round as breasts
dressed
    in apple leaves.

How to Make Plum Dumplings

        Pluck them
purple under dusky coats,
    polish against thigh,
            take a bite—

        Ah. Now hold
the stoneware bowl
    swollen with gems
            to your breast,

        sit on the porch,
inhale the bluing-
    to-indigo sky,
            invite

        twilight to your table,
lap spilling over
    with ovals. With one
            arced flick,

        liberate the pit,
(leave the skin),
    heal again whole.
            Center in dough,

        fold corners,
massage between palms
    until seamless, smooth.
            Drop into blue

        enameled pot, flame hot,
flesh yielding, skin
    bleeding its night shade
            crimson to aubergine—

   breathe in steam.
When risen, tender,
  slip from water,
     christen

    in crumb and butter,
lover, in cinnamon sugar,
  and a lick
     of cream.

Untitled, with Valentine

A bowl of figs, honey
comb of a pomegranate we
didn't eat with brie and wine.
I still wear the heart
you gave me, dried flowers

cobwebbed in the vase
Gospel of Thomas
on the chair's brown arm.
How much time between days
the track of a decade

gone, the arrival of another
milestone within our grasp.
There is a house beyond
a pasture, two horses, grass
grown over. There is a house

I've been to and never seen.
A view of the mountains, a loft
a spring. These trees hide it
all so well. I know
you must be home.

Distracted

  From ground mellowed
by a leafy infusion of alder
    and Western maple,
        buttercup and dandelion surrender
  almost willingly to my grasp.

  I clip forsythia,
whose reaching arms drew
    replicas of itself on the lawn
      last summer, and once-
  stunted Japanese maple

  shadows white viburnum stars.
Navigating waves of foliage
    I rediscover the concrete fish
      that swims in yellow lilies.
  Miscanthus Variegata,

to 4', full sun, is choked
amidst salal and clumps
    of pasture grass, planted
      when we dreamed of sheep.
  Warm sun weaves

  through raspberry thimbles,
makes me consider
    quitting the pulling, piling
      of weeds to reach for
  the book I left under the apple tree

>   but here you come,
> down the driveway
>   in your blue truck, and I think
>   I'll go in, make us a sandwich
>   instead.

Take Bread Away From Me If You Wish

—after a line by Pablo Neruda

  A baker once told me
you are an old soul

    Is this life my last attempt

        at rising?
                Dear baker

    I walked with the ocean
beneath the starting stars

      wild yeast of waves
holding my pan of loneliness

   phantom loaf—

❋ ❋ ❋

   This morning
you said we needed more
        bread—wheat—
   and I agreed

   to oatmeal and molasses
stick of butter
        to fatten us both.
We've abstained

from kneading
so long we gorge in dreams.
        By the woodstove
you feed the *biga*

   until it bubbles, while I
put my trust in honey
        a little rye.
What our hands make

   takes a night
   a day.

Woman Emerges From Mud

Chip of sandstone in your palm,
   you find a willing seam,
slide a blade until it widens.
    Separate the layers — whorl
      of red and ochre inside.

Other stones disclose slender stems,
   nuts of trees long extinct.
Trace the serrated edges of leaves,
   tiny bones of a life trapped
     when mud rushed over restless earth.

      Imagine yourself
      caught in an instant —

picking berries, tracking antelope,
   pursued by bear or boar,
when terra thunders underfoot.
    The warning roar, darkening sky.
    Sun swallowed in dust.

     How your body burns
     after the world ceases its chatter.

Imagine opening your dormant life,
   layers flaking away.
You, rescued by a knife
   slicing into stone, your first gasp
    the astonishing brightness of night.

House of Sweet Figs

The time I turned into mourning ash
I thought I was glimmering
I believed resurrection

meant having to swim
through bitter fruit   Sometimes
I wrestled with hornets

Once   I gathered nest after nest
until my fingers bled
I wore grief

until light bested me   There
radiance stung and I
ripened   I bruised

past clouds and they reminded me
of breath   sadness   flesh
How else would we have met?

My future was wound
loosely   and I   raveled

a paring of smoke

The Halo of You Was Pulled Apart

Days I chip my obsidian skin
Say bulb of percussion   say flint

Be sparrow   unsparing of word

I have these boxes :   of bleeding heart
tulips   of daffodils

Little halos gravity-torn

Each night my red fist pulses in my ear
Each night I say no

Grandmother I delay you   Let's return

to pounding spearheads   to ribs
unhinging   the snap and separation

of sparrows   The tulip loves

its little fist   Sometimes
I see in soil   little souls   splinters

of halo   Moon rise at noon

It's been thirteen years   Grandmother
the homily promised lamplight

said artist   said shapeshift

I keep these specimens boxed
In spring I plant you again

Eve in Winter

    At daybreak
something prattles
  in the apple tree.

  Peering through naked
winter light, barely I see
      the one who speaks —

      he is a leaf that never fell,
or the idea of a leaf,
  a black foreshadowing.

  Beneath branches a cat chatters,
sees angels as chickadees.
     I saw one once,

     what was left,
its feathers a scatter of ash
  on my porch.

  Cradled in a trowel,
I placed its weightlessness
     under maple leaves.

    Next day I found
it'd flown away, taking with it
  its single wing.

Postcard From the Lighthouse

This is only to let you know I've arrived.
I've closed the holes on the shore with my foot-
steps & left the sleeping pup to sun. Today
an eagle shed its quill & with it I write you that
I wrested an abalone ear from the many-
fingered kelp. That I've scrawled in sand
mustn't alarm you — the Hunter's Moon
erases all faults with its blood.

You Tell Me Happiness May Not Be Communicable

—after a line by Mike White

yet there are otters beneath my feet.
There are dogs on the sand.

An eagle sweeps the sky of rain
and I wonder, have you seen

the exhale of eel grass, beached
carrion calling each crow

Come, eat, this is my body
given for you. One fine

corvus brachyrhynchos selects
a crab leg, flies it to her mate.

I have a camera.
I have all day.

She has let the leg drop.
He consoles; they are so close.

There are clouds no one knows the names of.
There are many ways to arrive.

Housewife Shifts Her '64 Ford Galaxie into Hyperdrive

                She blazes home
      round the corner of
darkness and dawn, smoking
        tires blown to shreds
              in shapes of quasars
        and supernovas.
  Moon shells dance
a comet trail on her dash.
      She's got a stash of
            seeds in a sack
       under the seat.
  She doesn't see
when she is seen, she writes
      while driving, her children
           in constant dis-
        composure. She knows
    exposure to gas clouds
and house dust
      may spawn planets.
                When the moon cracks
        she scatters ashes
  over the garden
little rings around the Cosmos
      prayer for bright flowers
            shock of stars.

I Leave You the Cosmos

arcing for light under dark

wrap of jasmine.
I leave you early

fireworks crackling, snap
peas lengthening, the honeyed

sun. I leave you quickening
to twig crack, black

bird rasp, coyotes' maniacal
laugh. I leave you

September's half-eaten moon.
I leave you barely

fledged.
I leave you fallen

apples in sacks, green,
unblushed, blistered & cracked.

One tree of hard luck, three
seasons of bruised fruit.

Putting the Garden to Bed

The beanpoles are naked now,
the last summer vegetables collected in baskets.
I pull popweed and dandelion, feeling the easy slide,
gentle rip of roots through fertile earth. I stand,
gloved hands resting on the pitchfork, to watch

strings once holding snap peas dance on the breath
of October winds. Once draped with thick vines
of pregnant pods, the children's teepee, now stripped,
stands within picking distance of their empty
wading pool. On warm days "pea boats" floated
    on reflected water.

My pantry now crowded with pints of green beans
canned with cloves of garlic, red pepper flakes,
mustard seeds. Bottles of strong black and raspberry
cordials, sweet jams, jars of spiced applesauce fill
newly made pine shelves. In light rain

I exchange pitchfork for clippers, cut pumpkins,
still green, from thick umbilical vines.
Removing dying leaves I search for the snake
that crawled into my garden to die.
I discovered it in early summer, lying motionless
under shady leaves, and I touched it, wanting

to see it glide in circular motion, over and under itself.
But its body had already begun to shrink inward.
I imagine now that death really hasn't claimed it,
that it has slipped gracefully away, over and under,
to some other Eden.

About the Author

Ronda Broatch is the author of *Shedding Our Skins*, (Finishing Line Press, 2008) and *Some Other Eden*, (2005). Her journal publications include: *Atlanta Review*, *RHINO*, *Prairie Schooner*, *Fourteen Hills*, *Mid-American Review*, and *Fire On Her Tongue: An Anthology of Contemporary Women's Poetry* (Two Sylvias Press). Seven-time Pushcart Prize nominee, Ronda is the recipient of an Artist Trust GAP Grant, and was a May Swenson Poetry Award finalist four years running.

A Seattle native, Ronda is a graduate of the University of Washington, receiving degrees in Creative Writing, Photography, and Art, and has had the good fortune to study poetry with Nelson Bentley, and short story writing with Charles Johnson. She has taught poetry workshops to students from grade school to high school level, and has been a mentor for West Sound Academy's literary magazine, Mud Pie. Her photography has appeared in local galleries, including the Gallery At Grace, (Grace Episcopal Church, Bainbridge Island).

Ronda edits the literary journal *Crab Creek Review* and teaches a variety of fitness classes at the Poulsbo Athletic

Club. Starting with Poetry Month three years ago, she began a tradition of reading a poem every Tuesday to her Silver Sneakers Yoga class.

www.ingramcontent.com/pod-product-compliance
Lightning Source LLC
Chambersburg PA
CBHW021442080526
44588CB00009B/646